CONTENTS

MARVELING AT MARSUPIALS

One day when I was thirteen years old, I heard a knock on the door. I answered it to find one of my dad's biology students standing with a shoebox in his hands. "Here," he said, giving me the box. I cautiously peeked under the lid to discover the bulging bright eyes of a baby opossum staring back at me. Delighted, I picked up the tiny, furry form. I made a home for her in one of my dresser drawers and, during the next three months, raised her by feeding her baby food. At least for a while, we became best friends. I didn't understand at the time just how special my new companion was.

My baby opossum belonged to a unique group of mammals called marsupials. Earth is home to about three hundred marsupial species. Most live in Australia, New Guinea, and South America. They include kangaroos, koalas, and wombats—some of our planet's most beloved and unusual animals.

Marsupials have astonished people for centuries. Captain James Cook, the first European to explore eastern Australia, eagerly described his first look at a kangaroo in 1770. He concluded that "it bears no sort of resemblance to any European animal I ever saw." Today, tourists from all over the world still flock to Australia to catch a glimpse of a kangaroo hopping through a field or a koala sitting in a tree. Marsupials are definitely worth the attention.

But what are they?

A baby opossum, very much like mine, wanders through the grass.

THE IN-BETWEEN MAMMALS

Biologists classify mammals into three distinct groups. The first group is the *monotremes,* which includes the platypus and echidnas. The second group is the *eutherian,* or placental, mammals. Eutherians include most of the mammals we are familiar with—from cats and dogs to elephants, whales, rats—and, of course, people. Opossums, kangaroos, koalas, and wombats belong to the third group of mammals, the *metatherians,* or marsupials.

Three Kinds of Mammals

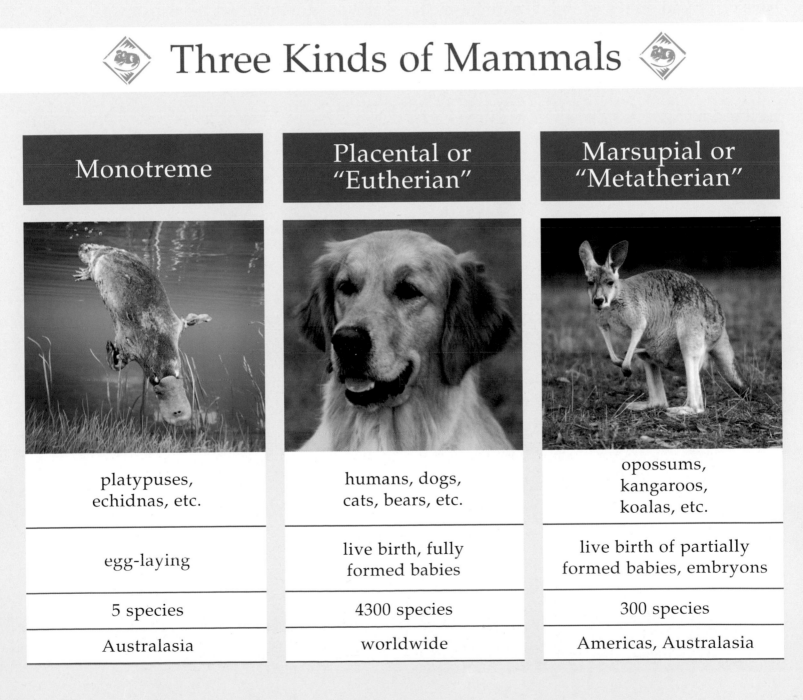

Monotreme	Placental or "Eutherian"	Marsupial or "Metatherian"
platypuses, echidnas, etc.	humans, dogs, cats, bears, etc.	opossums, kangaroos, koalas, etc.
egg-laying	live birth, fully formed babies	live birth of partially formed babies, embryons
5 species	4300 species	300 species
Australasia	worldwide	Americas, Australasia

ALIKE AND DIFFERENT

All three groups of mammals—monotremes, placentals, and marsupials—share common features. All are warm-blooded, which allows them to function efficiently in a wide range of temperatures. All mammals also bear *mammary glands* that produce milk for their young. Most mammals are covered in hair and have advanced senses of sight, hearing, smell, and touch. Mammals also are very intelligent, compared to other animal groups.

However, when it comes to reproducing, or making babies, the three groups of mammals couldn't be more different. Monotremes—the platypus and the echidna—lay eggs. Eutherian mammals—including people—give birth to fully formed babies. In between the monotremes and the eutherians are the marsupials.

LIVING ON THE OUTSIDE

Unlike the other two mammal groups, marsupials give birth to partially formed babies. After an egg is fertilized, the embryo stays inside the mother's body only for a short period of time. Within a few days, or a couple of weeks at most, this barely formed creature—called an *embryon*—leaves the mother's womb and undertakes a short, dangerous journey to a nipple. Here, the embryon attaches and begins feeding outside of the mother's body. Often—but not always—the nipple is protected in a special *pouch* or pocket. Safe in this pouch, the embryon nurses and grows until it is ready to begin exploring and feeding on its own.

Marsupials make up only about seven percent of the world's mammal species, but they have evolved into a wonderful variety of shapes and sizes, with a fascinating array of habits and features. To understand them completely, though, it's useful to know where they came from.

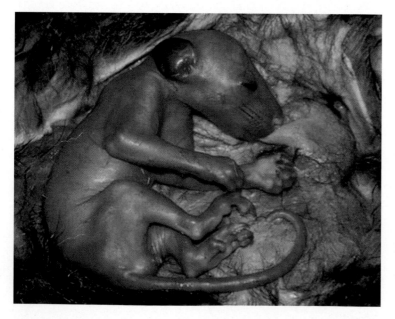

Kangaroos, and all other marsupials, have partially formed embryons that attach to an outside mammary gland of the mother and continue to develop into fully formed baby animals. This is a kangaroo embryon, safe inside its mother's pouch.

THE RISE OF THE MARSUPIALS

The story of marsupials begins with the evolution of the world's first mammals, three to four hundred million years ago. These first mammals remain mysterious. Scientists don't know who their ancestors were. They also aren't sure exactly when mammals split into the three major groups—the monotremes, placentals, and marsupials. Until recently, fossil evidence suggested that marsupials first evolved in North America and spread out from there. But in 2003, scientists reported finding in China the fossil of a marsupial that was 125 million years old—older than any marsupial that had been found in North America or anywhere else. Scientists named the animal *Sinodelphys szalayi* (sine-o-DEL-fis za-LAY-eye).

This fossil find suggests that the first marsupials evolved not in North America, but in Asia.

If that is true, how did they get to South America and Australia—places that are separated from Asia by thousands of miles of ocean?

The answer lies in the continents.

The fossil of *Sinodelphys szalayi* that was found in China.

© Mark Hallett

This is an artist's concept of what the prehistoric marsupial, *Sinodelphys szalayi*, may have looked like.

Scientists rely on two major tools to help unravel the history of life on Earth. One is *fossil evidence*. Since life began, some animals have been trapped and preserved in Earth's sediments. Their hard, or bony, parts get replaced with hard minerals that preserve their shape and form. By comparing fossils with the rocks they are found in, scientists can get a pretty good idea of how old different fossils are. They can also make good guesses about the possibility of two animals being closely related, but this is a bit tricky. Some close relatives look very different from each other. Manatees, for instance, don't look anything like elephants, but the two share a close common ancestor. On the other hand, animals that are *not* closely related can look very much alike. The thylacine (see "Extinct and Endangered," page 58) looks very much like a modern coyote, but the two are only distantly related.

To help them pin down animal relationships, scientists rely on a second tool called *DNA evidence*. DNA is contained in the living cells of every organism, and it provides instructions about how an organism develops, what it looks like, and even how it behaves. Changes in DNA over time create new adaptations and even new species.

By comparing the DNA from two different organisms, scientists can get an idea of how closely related those organisms are. If two species of monkeys have DNA that is very similar, scientists know that they share a more recent common ancestor. If the monkeys' DNA differs a lot, that means that the two species split off from each other much longer ago.

Both fossil and DNA evidence have their shortcomings. Fossil evidence is often hard to find and is usually incomplete. DNA evidence can only be gathered from living organisms, or in some cases, from soft body parts that have been preserved. Taken together, however, these two kinds of evidence give scientists a good picture of how today's organisms evolved.

manatee

elephant

thylacine

coyote

CONTINENTAL HOPSCOTCH

One hundred twenty-five million years ago, all of the continents were joined to form two supercontinents called Laurasia and Gondwana. Laurasia consisted of today's Asia, Europe, and North America. Gondwana was made up of Africa, South America, Australia, and Antarctica. If marsupials first evolved in Asia, they would have easily spread throughout North America and Europe. However, because Laurasia and Gondwana were separated by water, marsupials would *not* have been able to reach any part of Australia, South America, Africa, or Antarctica.

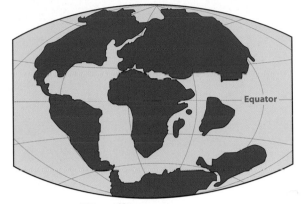

70 million years ago

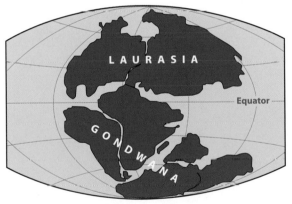

125 million years ago

But continents are not anchored in place. They float around on enormous pieces of Earth's crust called *continental plates*. Today, for instance, the Australian plate is drifting toward Asia at the rate of about two-and-a-half inches each year. That may not seem like much, but when you consider that earth is *billions* of years old, the continents have been zipping along like geological speedboats! This movement, called *continental drift*, allowed marsupials to dramatically extend their range.

By seventy million years ago, Africa had left Gondwana and drifted into Europe and Asia, allowing marsupials to spread into Africa. More important, South America had drifted over and hooked up with North America. According to mammal specialists Michael Archer and John Kirsch, this new land link allowed marsupials to invade South America between sixty-three million and seventy million years ago. From South America, marsupials kept moving. They followed land links into Antarctica, and from there, into Australia.

And the marsupial story was just beginning.

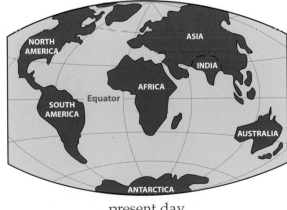

present day

Major Marsupial Events in Prehistoric Times

125 to 70 Million Years Ago

Marsupials evolve in Asia, eventually reaching Europe and North America.

75 to 45 Million Years Ago

Marsupials spread from North America to South America; from there, they spread to Antarctica and Australia; marsupials also spread to Africa from Asia/Europe.

NORTH AMERICA

EUROPE

ASIA

AFRICA

SOUTH AMERICA

AUSTRALIA

ANTARCTICA

45 to 5 Million Years Ago

Marsupials go extinct in North America, Asia, Europe, and Africa; meanwhile, they thrive and undergo spectacular radiation in South America and Australia.

5 Million Years Ago

North and South America reconnected via the Panamanian land bridge, leading to the extinction of many South American marsupials.

EXTINCTION AND RADIATION

The marsupials that invaded South America, Antarctica, and Australia began evolving into many different species. Scientists call this process *adaptive radiation* or *speciation*. South America, for instance, gave rise to large marsupials that resembled bears and saber-toothed tigers. At a site called Riversleigh in Australia, scientists have unearthed an amazing variety of fossil marsupials, including nine-foot-tall kangaroos, marsupial lions, and ancestors of today's koalas.

Meanwhile, the marsupials of North America, Africa, and Asia were having some problems. Here, eutherian, or placental, mammals began out-competing marsupials and eventually drove every last one of them to extinction. In the southern hemisphere, disasters also struck. Between three and five million years ago, eutherian mammals—and perhaps giant carnivorous birds—swept into South America over the Panamanian land bridge. These new arrivals eliminated many—but not all—of South America's marsupials.

The marsupials in Antarctica fared even worse. As Antarctica floated south, ice covered the entire continent, wiping out marsupials—and most other animals, too.

Only in Australia, far from any other continent, did marsupials enjoy a favorable climate without competition from other major mammal groups. Some eutherian mammals did manage to reach Australia, but they didn't prevent the native marsupials from evolving into an amazing array of species—including many of the remarkable forms we see today.

Before meeting the more famous Australian forms, however, let's take a look at the marsupials we can find closer to home.

NEW WORLD MARSUPIALS: OPOSSUMS O'PLENTY

In the past, it is likely that more marsupials lived in the Americas than today—a lot more! At one time, South America was home to six different orders of marsupials. Three of those orders became extinct. However, three "New World" marsupial orders still survive. These orders contain three living families and about one hundred living species. Most inhabit South America, but over time, some have traveled north to invade Central America and Mexico. One species, the Virginia opossum, has spread all the way up into Canada.

Together, these New World marsupials are an amazing bunch of critters. "The first thing that pops into my mind about New World marsupials is diversity," explains mammalogist Ron Pine. Dr. Pine has a special interest in American marsupials and has spent decades collecting and studying them.

"Everybody knows that the Australian marsupials are very diverse," says Dr. Pine, "but most people have no idea *how* diverse the New World marsupials are. They come in all different shapes, sizes, and colors."

A look at the opossums proves his point.

New World European-Style

"New World" refers to the continents of North and South America and nearby islands. "Old World" refers to all other parts of our planet that were known to Europeans before the voyages of Christopher Columbus. These include Europe, Africa, and Asia. The terms "New World" and "Old World" came from Europeans, who didn't know until the fifteenth century that the Americas existed. To them, North and South America were a new world, and these terms are still widely used today.

NORTH AMERICA

SOUTH AMERICA

New World Marsupial Families

Family Name	Common Name	Number of Species
(1) *Didelphidae*	opossums	90+
(2) *Caenolestidae*	shrew opossums or rat opossums	6
(3) *Microbiotheridae*	monito del monte	1

Didelphidae: opossums

Caenolestidae: shrew opossums or rat opossums

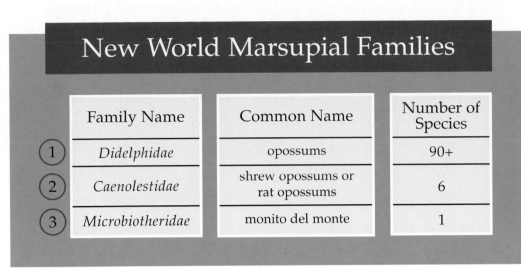

Microbiotheridae: monito del monte

HOW SCIENTISTS GROUP LIVING THINGS

Scientists group living things according to a strict naming, or *classification*, system, beginning with large groups and getting smaller—and more closely related. Living things, for instance, are lumped into really large groups called *kingdoms*. Marsupials and all other animals are in the *animal kingdom*, all plants are in the *plant kingdom*, and so forth. Below the level of kingdom are (in order): *phylum*, *class*, *order*, *family*, and finally, *genus* and *species*. There are also sub-groupings such as *subphylum*, *subclass*, and *suborder*.

Usually, scientists do not write down every scientific group a living thing belongs to. For example, the scientific name *Didelphis virginiana* refers only to the genus and species name of the Virginia opossum, but the full classification of this animal looks like this:

Kingdom: Animalia
Phylum: Chordata
Class: Mammalia
Order: Didelphimorphia
Family: Didelphidae
Genus: Didelphis
Species: *Didelphi virginiana*

This looks like a nice, neat system—but, reader, beware! The scientific classification system is *not* perfect. Scientists often disagree on how living things are related. One scientist might think that a certain Australian possum belongs in one family; another scientist might assign that same possum to another family. Scientific thinking is constantly changing—and so are scientific names—as scientists learn more about Earth's living things. That's part of what makes scientific discovery so exciting and interesting.

People are fascinated by marsupials, but most of us have some mistaken beliefs about them. To test your knowledge of marsupials, ask yourself if the following statements are **true** or **false**.

Myth #1: "All marsupials have pouches."

While it's true that the more famous marsupials have pouches, many do not. In the opossums, for instance, pouches have evolved in the larger species, while many smaller species remain pouchless.

baby Virginia opossum

pouchless mouse opossum

Myth #2: "The Virginia opossum is the only marsupial living outside of the Australian region."

The Americas are home to not one, but about one hundred species of marsupials. Papua New Guinea and several other Pacific islands also have marsupials.

Myth #3: "All opossums are ugly, slow, and stupid."

While the Virginia opossum may not be the most attractive animal on Earth, many opossums are beautiful, fast, and intelligent. Even the Virginia opossum is an intelligent animal and can "make tracks" when it's in a hurry. And baby Virginia opossums are real cuties!

Myth #4: "Marsupials are the only mammals native to Australia."

Australia is famous for marsupials, but it is also home to native monotremes (the platypus and echidna), native bats, and a whole raft of native rodents.

THE OPOSSUMS

By far the greatest number of New World marsupials belongs in the family *Didelphidae* (die-DEL-fi-dee), or the opossums. So far, scientists have identified more than ninety species of opossums, and they discover new species on a regular basis.

Many people living in the United States are familiar with the Virginia opossum, *Didelphis virginiana*. This is the animal that climbs into our garbage cans and seems to have a special talent for getting run over by cars. The Virginia opossum has a reputation for being slow, clumsy, and—let's face it—ugly. This reputation is not entirely fair, but it has made many people believe that all opossums are awkward, distasteful animals.

Nothing could be further from the truth.

"The great majority of the New World marsupials are beautiful, charming, lovely, cute little creatures," Ron Pine explains. "Many are delicate animals with big eyes and big, crinkly ears. They have little sharp faces with long whiskers and soft, woolly fur."

Opossums range in size from animals as small as mice to big animals, such as our "heavyweight," the Virginia opossum, which can weigh ten pounds and stretch thirty-one inches from its nose to the tip of its tail. Opossums occupy deserts and grasslands, but

their spread-out toes and grasping, or *prehensile*, tails make most of them especially suited to climbing the trees and bushes.

Opossums can use their prehensile tails for hanging onto branches.

THE VIRGINIA OPOSSUM: A CLOSER LOOK

Even though the Virginia opossum is the United States' and Canada's only native opossum, it doesn't exactly have the best reputation. Maligned for being slow, unsightly, and dim-witted, the opossum would be about the last critter to star in its own movie or television show.

Part of the Virginia opossum's bad reputation comes from the fact that the opossums—like many other animals—freeze up in the headlights of oncoming cars and trains. This makes people wrongly assume that the animals are stupid. Those who know these animals, though, believe they deserve a much better reputation.

"At the St. Louis Zoo," curator Alice Seyfried explains, "we have a show opossum, Roland, that we use in one of our shows. He's quite trainable. He comes out of one stage door and walks across the stage and over a little pile of wood to get a food reward. Then he goes down a little pile of logs and through the other stage door. He's a pretty smart little opossum."

Opossums' "hands" help them climb.

A group of young opossums are safe up high in a tree.

Virginia opossums also have other positive features. "They're very clean," says Seyfried. "We never have to groom them, because they groom themselves. They're very particular about where they go to the bathroom in their enclosures. They've also adapted very well to the changes in their surroundings."

The opossum has an especially neat method of dealing with predators. When faced with a dangerous predator, the opossum "plays dead"—a trick that often convinces the predator to look for a livelier meal. Virginia opossums have been so successful at adapting to their environments that they've spread throughout most of the United States and into Canada. No other marsupial can say *that!*

 # The Virginia Opossum

The Virginia opossum is not a stupid animal. In fact, it has learned many different ways to survive when threatened. It may run, growl, belch, urinate, or even defecate to frighten its attacker.

Its most famous defense, though, is to "play possum," pretending to be dead. The animal will roll over, become stiff, and even drool. Most predators prefer live meals, so they usually move on. Opossums can stay in this coma-like condition for up to four hours!

A growling opossum can scare away a predator.

When an opossum "plays possum," its attacker loses interest.

Behaving Like an Opossum

Even though scientists have identified ninety or more different species of opossums, we know very little about most of them. "For many of these things," Dr. Pine says, "we know *absolutely nothing* about their habits. All we know about is what measurements you get when you measure their little skulls and how many bumps they have on their teeth and facts like that."

Opossums climb well because they have opposable thumbs that help them grab hold and hang on.

Still, we do know some things. Most opossums are *nocturnal* (active at night) and are usually highly secretive. They are also good eaters. "Opossums in general will eat anything that is edible and that they can get their mouth around," Dr. Pine says. Some opossums survive on diets of insects or hunt lizards, snails, and other small animals. Many—if not all—are *omnivorous*, eating fruit, leaves, garbage, and even carcasses of other animals.

Some opossums probably have definite territories, but those that have been studied seem to be nomadic. They wander widely in search of food and mates. Along the way, they perform *scent marking* by rubbing objects with the sides of their heads, chins, or other body parts to leave behind "perfumes." Other opossums recognize these smells. Male Virginia opossums, for instance, can recognize individual females by these scents. Scent marking probably does not define a territory as it does for wolves or tigers, but it may help animals get to know each other before mating—and help warn other males to stay away.

MAKING MORE OPOSSUMS

Speaking of mating, some opossums breed throughout the year. Others breed only once per year. The Virginia opossum has two breeding seasons: one that peaks in February and another in early summer.

Opossums are well known for bearing large numbers of offspring. It's not uncommon to see an opossum with a dozen or more babies hanging from it. Virginia opossums typically have eight to ten babies but have been known to have more than twenty. One species, the southern red-sided opossum, *Monodelphis sorex*, comes equipped with up to twenty-seven nipples—the most of any known mammal.

Some opossums build nests. Others do not. Larger opossums, such as the Virginia opossum, have pouches in which the young are carried. But smaller opossums, including the gray short-tailed opossum, do not have pouches at all.

Whether they have access to a pouch or not, the young must stay attached to their mother's nipples for a period of several weeks to several months. If they fall off during this period, they won't be able to reattach, and they will die. As they grow larger, however, the babies start leaving the nipples and crawling up onto the mother's back.

Certain opossum mothers are better than others. The Robinson's mouse opossum, *Marmosa robinsoni*, will retrieve a pup if it has fallen off. However, if a baby Virginia opossum falls off its mother, the mother will not make any effort to retrieve it, and the baby will die. Even from a large litter, only three or four opossum babies usually survive to head out on their own.

But to really understand opossums, we need to meet a few of them, face to whiskered face.

What Do You Call a Baby Marsupial?

When they are first born, most baby marsupials are tiny, naked, pink creatures. It's no surprise that at this stage they are sometimes called "pinkies." What they are called after that depends on where they are. Baby Australasian marsupials in general are known as "joeys." Baby American marsupials are simply referred to as the "young" or "babies" or "pups."

WET OPOSSUMS

The water opossum, *Chironectes minimus* (kie-roc-NEK-tees MIN-i-muss), has a lifestyle different from all other opossums. "They are beautiful animals to begin with," Ron Pine explains. "They have this marvelous, soft, dense, woolly fur and pretty gray coloration. They have big, dark brown—almost black—saddles on their backs and an immaculate white belly."

However, it's the water opossum's habits that make it stand out. The territory of the water opossum ranges from Argentina all the way up into southern Mexico. Unlike any other known opossum, it hunts primarily in shallow streams. It has large hind feet that are webbed like a duck's and special rough pads on its very sensitive front feet, or hands. Dr. Pine explains, "They swim around with their front feet stuck straight out in front and paddle with their webbed hind feet so they can they feel things with their hands. That tells them whether or not something is good to eat."

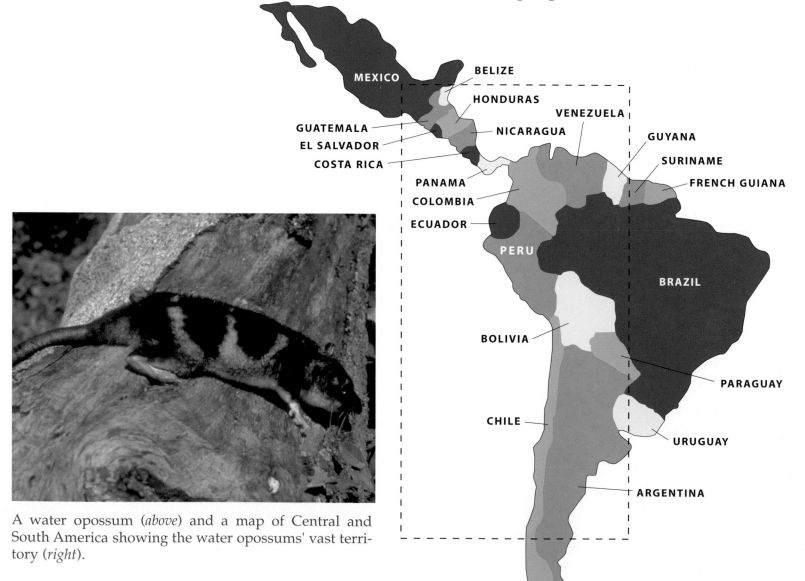

MEXICO
BELIZE
HONDURAS
VENEZUELA
GUATEMALA
NICARAGUA
GUYANA
EL SALVADOR
SURINAME
COSTA RICA
FRENCH GUIANA
PANAMA
COLOMBIA
ECUADOR
PERU
BRAZIL
BOLIVIA
PARAGUAY
CHILE
URUGUAY
ARGENTINA

A water opossum (*above*) and a map of Central and South America showing the water opossums' vast territory (*right*).

SHORT-TAILED OPOSSUMS

An equally interesting opossum is the yellow-sided opossum, *Monodelphis dimidiata* (mo-no-DEL-fis di-mi-dee-AW-tuh). Yellow-sided opossums are about the size of a Chinese hamster and belong to a group called the short-tailed opossums. They do not live in forests as most opossums do, but instead make their homes in grasslands near streams where they feed largely on insects.

What's so fascinating about these animals is that they live for only about one year. "At a given time in the fall," says Ron Pine, "there's only one generation around, and they're all the same age. They're all babies. They remain small throughout the winter when there isn't much food. Then, in spring, they start to grow like crazy. However, once the male opossums mate with the females, the males die. The females raise the young. Then, after the young have been weaned, the females also die."

This raises the question: Why do the adults die so quickly? According to Dr. Pine, this might be an adaptation to living in a fairly extreme environment. For an adult, finding enough food to stay alive through the winter may be an impossible task. Babies, on the other hand, require much less food and are probably able to survive better through the long "foodless" season. Having the adults die also prevents them from competing with their young for limited food supplies.

The South American short-tailed opossum, *Monodelphis domestica*, is a near relative to the yellow-sided opossum.

THE WOOLLY OPOSSUMS

Some especially enchanting Didelphids are the woolly opossums (*below right*). There are three species, and they are *arboreal*, meaning they live in trees. Woolly opossums are exceptionally beautiful. They also are known for their speed and agility. They climb and leap through forests in search of fruit, insects, leaves, and other food to eat. I encountered one in Costa Rica that was also quite curious. It stared at me for almost a minute, studying me, perhaps wondering what I was up to.

A shrew, or rat, opossum has fleshy flaps of skin on its lips.

A woolly opossum hangs onto a branch at night.

MEET THE FLAP-LIPS

Even though the Didelphids are the most dominant family of New World marsupials, they are not the only ones. A second family, the *Caenolestidae* (see-no-LES-tid-ee), includes about six species that together are called shrew opossums or rat opossums (*above left*). Dr. Pine thinks a better name would be the "flap-lips" because these animals have loose, fleshy flaps of skin on both sides of their lips. Caenolestids live in cool, wet habitats in South America, and they eat insects, spiders, centipedes, earthworms, and some plant matter. A distinctive feature of caenolestids is that their two bottom front incisors are long and stick straight out. They may use these strange teeth to impale their prey.

THE GONDWANA LINK

The third and last family of living New World marsupials is the *Microbiotheridae* (mi-kro-bi-o-THEER-i-dee), and it has only one living species, *Dromiciops australis* (dro-MEE-see-ops aw-STRAL-iss). In Spanish, it is called the *monito del monte*, which may be translated as "little monkey of the mountain" or "little monkey of the wild."

Dromiciops is a small marsupial with a body only four or five inches long. It is an excellent climber and lives in humid forests along the Andes Mountains in Chile and Argentina. Pairs of the animals make nests of leaves and sticks, which they line with grass or moss. Like many opossums, *Dromiciops* mainly eats insects and other arthropod invertebrates. Also, it appears to store fat in its tail—a feature shared by many other marsupials.

Scientists find *Dromiciops* especially interesting because of its surprising connection to its Australasian cousins. Scientists who have studied the DNA of all marsupials concluded that *Dromiciops* is much more closely related to many Australian marsupials than to other New World marsupials. This could mean two things. One is that Australian marsupials evolved from more than one wave of immigrants. Scientists generally believe that marsupials reached Australia by traveling through Antarctica from South America. It's possible, though, that different waves of marsupials entered Australia at different times. This is just another chapter that scientists hope to decode in their search for the complete marsupial story.

a baby monito del monte

an adult monito del monte

AUSTRALIASIAN MARSUPIALS: THE ANIMALS DOWN UNDER

As delightful as American marsupials are, it's those critters from *Australasia*—Australia, New Guinea, and nearby islands—that really blow most peoples' mammalian minds. Why? Australasia has twice as many marsupial species as North and South America. Even more important, these marsupials come in an astonishing variety of forms and have a boatload of remarkable behaviors.

Australasian marsupials are organized into four separate orders, but the most familiar one is the order Diprotodontia (die-pro-toe-DON-chuh). This order includes many of the world's most beloved mammals. Kangaroos, koalas, wombats, wallabies—Diprotodontia has them all. In fact, Diprotodontia is the world's largest marsupial order, containing 10 different families and at least 131 species.

The name "Diprotodontia" refers to the fact that all of these marsupials have two large lower incisor teeth that project forward. These unusual forward teeth allow Diprotodonts to "slice and dice" the grasses, leaves, and other plant materials they graze on. A second important feature of this group is that they are *syndactyl* (sin-DAK-tul). This means that the

second and third toes of the hind foot are joined together. No other group of marsupials has both of these features.

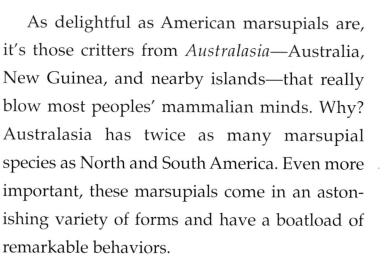

Macropodidae:
wallaby

Phascolarctidae:
koala

Vombatidae:
wombat

Potoroidae:
rat-kangaroo
(potoroo)

Phalangeridae:
cuscus

Acrobatidae:
feathertail glider

Burramyidae:
pygmy possums

Pseudocheiridae:
ringtail possum

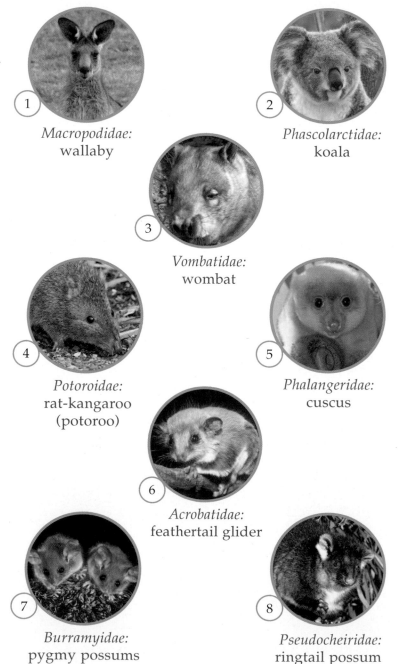

Petauridae:
sugar glider

Tarsipedidae:
honey possum

Notoryctidae:
marsupial mole

Peramelidae:
bilby

Peroryctidae:
spiny bandicoot

Dasyuridae:
Tasmanian devil

Myrmecobidae:
numbat

Thylacinidae:
thylacine

Australasian Marsupial Families

Order: Diprotodontia

	Family Name	Common Name	Number of Species
1	*Macropodidae*	kangaroos and wallabies	61+
2	*Phascolarctidae*	koala	1
3	*Vombatidae*	wombats	3
4	*Potoroidae*	rat-kangaroos	10+
5	*Phalangeridae*	cuscuses; brush-tail and scaly-tailed possums	22+
6	*Acrobatidae*	feathertail glider and feathertail possum	2
7	*Burramyidae*	pygmy possums	5
8	*Pseudocheiridae*	ringtail possums	16+
9	*Petauridae*	gliders and trioks	10+
10	*Tarsipedidae*	honey possum	1

Order: Notoryctemorphia

	Family Name	Common Name	Number of Species
11	*Notoryctidae*	marsupial mole	1+

Order: Peramelemorphia

	Family Name	Common Name	Number of Species
12	*Peramelidae*	bandicoots and bilbies	11
13	*Peroryctidae*	spiny bandicoots	11

Order: Dasyuromorphia

	Family Name	Common Name	Number of Species
14	*Dasyuridae*	quolls, Tasmanian devils, and others	17+
15	*Myrmecobidae*	numbat	1
16	*Thylacinidae*	thylacine or "Tasmanian tiger"	1 (extinct)

Kangaroos and Wallabies: The Big Feet

No matter how much you read about kangaroos, you can hardly believe they're real until you actually see one for yourself. All kangaroos and wallabies belong to the family Macropodidae (ma-kro-PO-di-dee), which means "big feet." At least sixty-one species of "big feet" live in Australia, New Guinea, and nearby islands. Many are impressive animals.

Consider the world's largest living marsupial, the red kangaroo, *Macropus rufus* (ma-kro-pus roo-fus). Males of this species may be almost six feet tall and weigh more than two hundred pounds. They have thick tails up to four feet long and large ears that constantly scan their surroundings for sounds of danger. Red kangaroos graze in open grasslands, usually in early morning, evening, and at night. What astonishes people most about these animals—and other macropods—is how they move.

A red kangaroo (*above*) and a wallaby (*below*) are both in the "big feet" family.

 ## Is it a kangaroo or a wallaby?

Kangaroos and wallabies are all macropods. The difference in names is based soley on their size. Large macropod species are called kangaroos. Small macropod species are called wallabies. You might ask, "What about macropods that are bigger than wallabies and smaller than kangaroos?" Well, Australians have a name for those, too. They are called wallaroos.

SPRING-LOADED

When foraging or advancing slowly, a red kangaroo moves with a comical "five-footed gait." Using its thick tail as a fifth foot, the animal balances on its tail and short front legs. Then it swings its large hind feet forward together.

It's at high speeds, though, that the red kangaroo really turns on the juice. When it wants to get somewhere fast, this marsupial bounds solely using its enormous hind legs. The main platform for this bounding is the animal's fourth toe, which has evolved to be extremely long. The kangaroo's leg tendons act like springs that store enormous amounts of energy. With such spring-loaded tendons, the kangaroo uses very little energy to leap enormous distances.

At full throttle, a large red kangaroo can cover almost thirty feet with each leap. It can cruise between fifteen and twenty miles per hour, with bursts exceeding forty miles per hour.

High fences? Not a problem. Dingoes or other predators? Eat my dust. But speed and size are not a kangaroo's only amazing features.

Kangaroos' tendons act like springs to help them jump far.

Here's a fact that will amuse your friends:

A group of kangaroos together is called a *mob*. Not all species form mobs. "Mob behavior" is found only in large species such as the red (*left*) and gray kangaroos (*above*).

Get in Line, Joey!

In addition to their remarkable appearance, kangaroos have an equally remarkable mode of reproduction. When a young embryo is born, it quickly crawls up into the mother's pouch and attaches to a nipple to begin getting nourishment to help it grow. Unlike other marsupials, however, most macropod mothers immediately mate again. Inside its mom's body, this second, new embryo grows to a size of only about one hundred cells. Then it stops growing. This is called *embryonic diapause*, or delayed birth. Only when the first embryo is weaned or dies does the second embryo resume growing, emerge from its mother's body, and make its way up to the pouch.

Embryonic diapause provides kangaroos with a backup plan in Australia's harsh environment. If the first offspring, or joey, perishes before it can mature, the mother already has a head start at raising a replacement. If the first joey survives, however, and conditions are good, the mother has a good shot at raising a second one. The downside of delayed birth is that a female 'roo is *always* pregnant. Ask your mom how she'd like that!

Pop Pouch Quiz!

Question: Do all pouches open in the same direction?

Pouches can open either toward the head or the tail of a marsupial. Kangaroos and many tree-climbing marsupials have forward-opening pouches. This keeps the joeys from flying out as Mom climbs trees or goes bounding across the Australian landscape. However, in wombats, water opossums, bandicoots, and many other pouched marsupials, the pouch opens toward the rear. For marsupials that burrow or swim, this orientation may keep dirt or water from getting into the pouch. Interestingly, the tree-climbing koala also has a rear-facing pouch. Scientists aren't sure why. It may be something that just never changed during the koala's evolution. But baby koalas also need to eat some of their mothers' feces, or poop, to get the special bacteria that allow the koala to digest tough eucalyptus trees. The koala's pouch may help out by placing baby face to face with this poop!

This is not a two-headed animal! A wombat's pouch faces the back.

Keeping Cool

In Australia's warm climate, keeping cool is especially important. Like other mammals, kangaroos sweat—but only while they are hopping. As soon as they stop hopping, they switch from sweating to panting.

Kangaroos have another fascinating cooling system, too. Their forearms are filled with tiny blood vessels. When a kangaroo licks its forearms, the moisture draws warmth out from the blood vessels and allows the heat to be carried away by the wind.

MACROPOD MULTITUDES AND TREE 'ROOS

At first glance, most macropods look like typical kangaroos—upright posture; big feet; long, thick tail; big ears. Upon closer inspection, however, various kinds of macropods start showing their many differences. Hare wallabies resemble rabbits or big, furry rats. Nail-tailed wallabies look extremely elegant, almost like two-footed gazelles. Some of the most intriguing—and beautiful—macropods are the tree kangaroos.

There are ten species of "tree 'roos" and, as their name suggests, they are specially adapted to live in rainforest trees of Australia and Papua New Guinea. Dr. Lisa Dabek works at Seattle's

A tree kangaroo sits in a favorite place—a tree!

Woodland Park Zoo and has studied tree kangaroos for decades.

"The hind legs of other kangaroos are extended and much longer than their forelegs," Dr. Dabek explains. "They can only hop, because their hind legs don't move independently. But tree kangaroos can actually move their hind limbs independently so they can climb as well as hop. They also have long forelimbs, not those little stubby ones that other kangaroos have. And they have long claws for climbing in the trees."

When it comes to reproduction, tree kangaroos are also different. Like other 'roos, they usually bear only one young at a time. This may be because of their diet of leaves, flowers, and other plant materials. These foods are hard to digest, so they produce less energy per bite. "What I found," explains Dr. Dabek, "is that because tree kangaroos are leaf-eaters, they have a fairly low metabolic rate, which slows down everything—including their reproduction."

Tree kangaroos are active both day and night. Despite their slow metabolism, they can move quickly through the forest. They sometimes come to the ground, but their bodies are built for climbing and leaping. One tree kangaroo was observed jumping down more than fifty feet to the ground without getting hurt!

Unlike some of the larger kangaroos, tree kangaroos tend to lead a solitary existence. "You'll see mothers and young," Dr. Dabek explains, "but the males only get together with females for breeding."

This is a grizzled grey tree kangaroo nibbling leaves in a tree. Notice its long forearms.

ROCK HOPPERS

Every bit as fascinating as tree kangaroos are the gorgeous animals known as rock wallabies. Scientists have identified at least fourteen species of rock wallabies. Adrienne Miller works at the Audubon Zoo in New Orleans and has traveled to Australia to work with one of the most endangered species of rock wallabies, the yellow-footed rock wallaby, *Petrogale xanthopus* (peh-tro-GAL-ee zan-tho-pus).

"They're incredibly beautiful," Miller says of the animals. "They have striped tails and orange feet—big, fuzzy feet. The pads on their feet are like SUV tires. They're all bumpy so they can really cling to the rocks. And, I mean, they can go straight up a rock wall without even making a sound."

Like other wallabies, the yellow-footed rock wallaby feeds mainly on grasses, flowering herbs, and shrubs—usually around dawn and dusk. They inhabit rocky outcrops and often live in groups of about one hundred individuals. "The rock wallabies are called 'colonial,'" explains Miller, "but I don't know whether they hang together by choice or because their environment has forced them together. There's no habitat they want to be in

The yellow-footed rock wallaby lives in groups on rocky terrain.

beyond their little rock area, so they might just be forced together because of that."

Most adult rock wallabies weigh between six and twenty pounds. They often have bold

Rock wallaby joeys are weaned very early.

stripes and other beautiful markings that made them a target for fur hunters in the past. Today, many of these animals are threatened by competition with introduced goats, sheep, and rabbits. Predation by introduced foxes and cats is also a problem—especially for the yellow-footed rock wallaby.

"For most marsupials," explains Miller, "the interval pouch life—the time from when the joey first comes out of the pouch to when it's permanently outside of the pouch—is a couple of months. But for the rock wallabies, it can be as short as a week. So the joeys actually get left alone very early, and that's one reason they succumb so easily to introduced predators. To survive, the joeys have to learn really, really fast."

Thumpin' and Gruntin'

Marsupials aren't famous for their noises. Many species do make grunting or coughing sounds during interactions, and mothers may click or cluck to call their young. But barking, howling, and bellowing? Forget it. However, pademelons and other social macropods are well known for thumping the ground with their big feet when danger is near. This rabbit-like behavior alerts their neighbors to get hopping and out of harm's way.

RAT-KANGAROOS: THE TREE PLANTERS

If you're ever camping in Queensland, Australia, and a little furry animal hops up to your tent looking for food, you may have just been visited by a rat-kangaroo. These rodent-like critters are not actually kangaroos, but they are close relatives. About ten species live in Australia, and they hop or shuffle around, mostly in forest habitats, eating fungi, fruit, seeds, and insects.

Some species of rat-kangaroos are also known as potoroos and bettongs. The largest weighs up to about seven pounds, and the smallest weighs only about a pound. Once considered pests because of their damage to potatoes and other crops, at least one species is now believed to serve a vital role in helping Australia's rainforests.

Biologist Andrew Dennis has conducted long-term studies on the musky rat-kangaroo, *Hypsirprymnodon moschatus* (hip-seer-prime-no-don mos-KAT-us). This diminutive species lives in the thick vegetation of tropical rain-forests, where it feeds primarily on the fruits and seeds of at least thirty-nine different plants. While observing the animals, Dennis discovered that, after plucking a fruit and nibbling on it, the rat-kangaroos often ran several yards away and buried the seed.

This behavior is called *caching*, and it is an animal's way of saving food for later—like woodpeckers storing acorns in tree holes. What's interesting is that the musky rat-kanga-roo never goes back to get most of the seeds that it buries. The result is that the creature accidentally plants new trees throughout the forest. Andrew estimates that these animals may plant up to four hundred seeds per acre! Without these busy gardeners, the future of many rain-forest plants might quickly wither away.

The musky rat-kangaroo is a natural tree planter.

KOALAS AND WOMBATS: THE UN-BEARS

Ask Australians what their favorite marsupials are, and koalas and wombats are sure to top the list. At first glance, the animals look remarkably similar—short, furry, stocky. It's understandable that both are often compared to bears. Until recently, in fact, the koala was usually called the "koala bear." Of course, neither the koala nor the wombat is related to bears, but that doesn't keep these marsupials from being fascinating creatures.

EATING AND SLEEPING: LIFE AS A KOALA

The koala is Australia's "poster child." Millions of visitors flock to Australia hoping to see these furry, outrageously cute little animals. What most people don't realize is that there is much more to this fascinating marsupial than its cuddly appearance.

Like tree kangaroos, koalas spend most of their lives in trees. But while tree kangaroos spend most of their time in rainforests, koalas inhabit Australia's drier forests of *eucalyptus trees*. Across their range, koalas have been observed making use of more than 120 species of eucalyptus. In fact, they depend almost entirely on eucalyptus leaves and bark for their food and shelter.

The koala could hardly have picked tougher plants to digest. While eucalyptus leaves may seem tender, they are full of woody fibers and

nasty chemicals. No worries, though. The koala has evolved an additional length of digestive tract to help it handle this tough, woody food.

Its eucalyptus diet yields so little nutrition that a koala must go to great lengths to conserve its energy. "Koalas sleep for twenty hours a day because of their low-nutrient diet," explains Dr. David Dique, the Principal Conservation Officer for Queensland's Environmental Protection Agency. Koalas are also nocturnal, so your chances of seeing one awake are, well, less than terrific.

But koalas can move quickly when they have to. During the mating season, a male may actively defend several females from the advances of other mates. Koalas can also scurry across the ground or up a tree when danger arises. Most koalas maintain a home range of between two and four acres, but in especially dry forests, home ranges can encompass up to one hundred acres.

It's All about Feet

Its soft fur, gentle eyes, and big ears make the koala appear "cuddly," but its feet are actually one of the koala's most fascinating features. Like other animals in the order Diprotodontia, the second and third toes of koala's hind feet are fused together. The koala also has a back "big toe" that functions just like a thumb. This "foot thumb" is called a *hallux* and is a feature shared by many other arboreal marsupials in both Australasia and the Americas.

The koala's front feet, or hands, are just as unusual as its hind feet. Instead of holding one digit to the side like a thumb, koalas hold two fingers on one side and three on the other. This forms a *V* pattern that, with the hallux, is ideally suited for climbing and grasping eucalyptus tree trunks and limbs.

sleeping koala

front foot, or "hand," of a koala

WOMBATS: LIVING CUBES WITH LEGS

Smart. Strong. Stubborn. Square. That pretty much sums up the wombat.

Three species of wombats live in different parts of Australia. They look like furry tractors with legs. Wombats are large animals, sometimes exceeding three feet in length and weighing more than eighty pounds. They tend to be shy but are compact and heavily muscled. This serves them well when they're busy with one of their favorite activities—burrowing.

Using their powerful, clawed front feet, wombats blast through even the hardest soil. They dig burrows up to one hundred feet long. Each burrow has only one entrance, but it may have many side tunnels below the surface.

Common wombats maintain territories of between ten and fifty acres, and they may dig a dozen or so burrows in different locations. Territories sometimes overlap, and occasionally two wombats may even share a burrow. But wombats generally keep to themselves.

a southern hairy-nosed wombat, one of the three wombat species

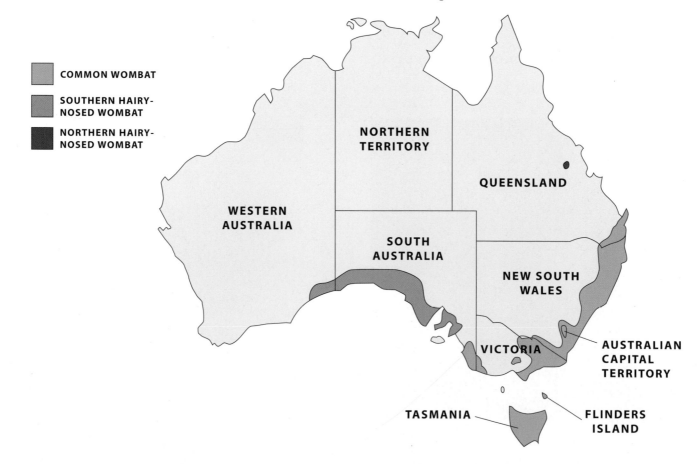

COMMON WOMBAT

SOUTHERN HAIRY-NOSED WOMBAT

NORTHERN HAIRY-NOSED WOMBAT

NORTHERN TERRITORY

QUEENSLAND

WESTERN AUSTRALIA

SOUTH AUSTRALIA

NEW SOUTH WALES

VICTORIA

AUSTRALIAN CAPITAL TERRITORY

TASMANIA

FLINDERS ISLAND

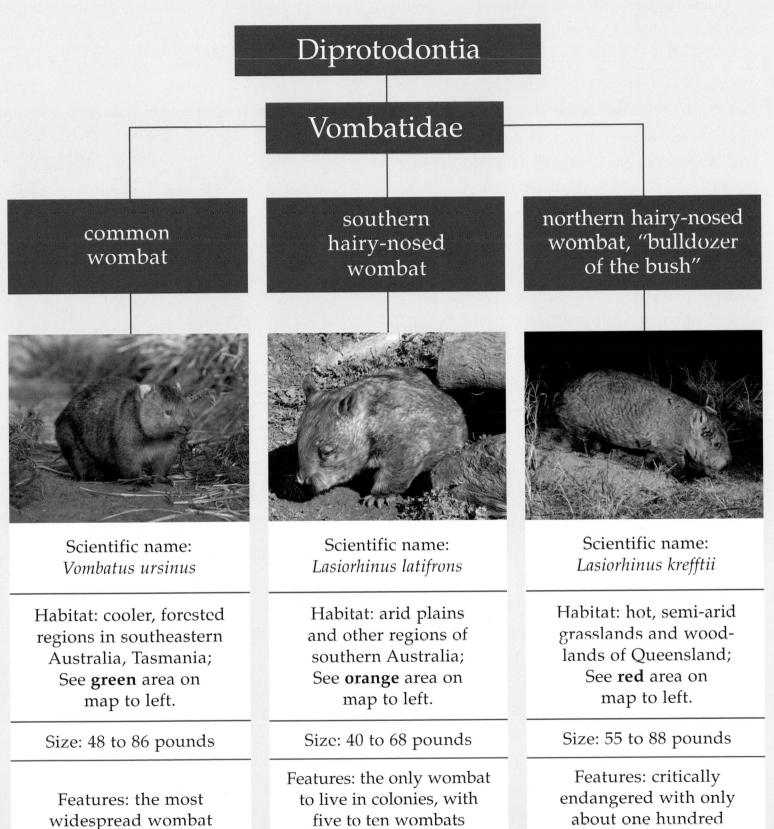

Diprotodontia

Vombatidae

common wombat	southern hairy-nosed wombat	northern hairy-nosed wombat, "bulldozer of the bush"
Scientific name: *Vombatus ursinus*	Scientific name: *Lasiorhinus latifrons*	Scientific name: *Lasiorhinus krefftii*
Habitat: cooler, forested regions in southeastern Australia, Tasmania; See **green** area on map to left.	Habitat: arid plains and other regions of southern Australia; See **orange** area on map to left.	Habitat: hot, semi-arid grasslands and wood-lands of Queensland; See **red** area on map to left.
Size: 48 to 86 pounds	Size: 40 to 68 pounds	Size: 55 to 88 pounds
Features: the most widespread wombat	Features: the only wombat to live in colonies, with five to ten wombats sharing one tunnel system	Features: critically endangered with only about one hundred animals surviving

HAVE TEETH, WILL EAT

Wombats are strict vegetarians. At night they emerge from their burrows to chow down tough grasses, roots, and fungi. They come equipped with some interesting tools to handle this tough diet. Like the teeth of horses and hippos, a wombat's teeth do not have roots. This enables them to continuously grow throughout the animal's life—a handy feature since grasses contain compounds called silicates that quickly grind down the wombat's teeth.

Like the koala's eucalyptus-leaf diet, the wombat's food is not very nutritious. Wombats have evolved a highly efficient digestive system to handle their protein-poor diet. Like the koalas, they also have a low metabolism, which reduces their need for food. A wombat eats only about one-third as much food as a kangaroo of the same size.

Wombats are not party animals. A typical wombat spends about three-quarters of its time resting in its burrows.

JOEYS, WHAT'S THE RUSH?

Wombats have only one or, at most, two offspring at a time. In years of drought, they often don't have any. This probably has to do with their sparse diet. To successfully raise young, wombats need every bit of food they can get.

Like the koala and many kangaroos, a baby wombat develops slowly. Once it enters the pouch, the joey will stay there until it is about eight months old, and it will not become fully weaned until age twelve months or so. Young wombats are not quick to "get out of the house," either. They stay with their moms for about two years—sometimes until Mom forces them to leave. In most other species, the young males disperse to new territories, but for wombats, the females are the ones that strike out on their own.

A young wombat ventures outside its mom's pouch.

UNPREDICTABLE PLAYMATES

They may not be the most active animals on the planet, but wombats have no trouble defending themselves. They kick at enemies with their strong back legs and will bite when necessary. Tamed wombats, though, have proven themselves to be pleasant companions.

Elaine Kirchner worked with wombats at the Fort Wayne (Indiana) Children's Zoo. "They were very playful, very determined animals," she recalls. "If they wanted to go someplace, they were like little tanks. They just bulldozed through it. But if one got out of its enclosure, all we had to do was lay a trashcan out, and she'd go running right into it. Once inside, she'd turn around, as if to say 'Hi! Here I am!'"

Elaine also discovered that wombats could get into mischief. When one wombat arrived at the zoo, Elaine and her co-workers placed her in a kitchen area until they could decide which pen to put her in. The next morning, Elaine walked in to find that the wombat had pulled four fifty-pound bags of food off the counter and onto the floor. "She'd chewed them all open and made herself a nest in the pile of food. She was very happy in there."

a wombat at the zoo

Name That Poop!

You don't have to be an expert in *scatology*—the study of excrement—to identify a wombat's poop. Wombats poop out dung that is almost perfectly cube-shaped. Their cube-shaped deposits nicely match wombats' cube-shaped bodies. The poops also have a special feature. When they harden, they can be used as building blocks!

A GRAB BAG OF POSSUMS AND CUSCUSES

The word "possum" has been applied to at least six families of marsupials in Australia and New Guinea. Most are cute, furry critters that have prehensile tails and—no surprise—live in trees. There are more than thirty species, far too many to describe here. But it is fun to climb around with a few of the "special" ones, along with some of their close relatives, the cuscuses.

THE AMAZING RE-APPEARING POSSUMS

Paleontologists have identified many extinct marsupials from bones and fossils. One of these was a little animal called the mountain pygmy possum, *Burramys parvus* (ber-AY-mis PAR-vus). This animal was thought to have disappeared after the Pleistocene Era, about fifteen thousand years ago. Then, in 1966, residents of a ski hut in Victoria, Australia, captured a small mouse-like animal. It turned out to be the "extinct" mountain pygmy possum!

Scientists discovered that this reappearing possum possesses many unusual features. For one thing, it is the only Australian mammal that lives in high mountain regions. Unlike most other possums, it does not live in trees but instead scurries across alpine meadows and boulder fields. It eats seeds, fruits, and worms but has a special appetite for bogong moths that migrate to the high mountain areas every year. It stores food to help it survive the tough winter months.

The mountain pygmy possum is a mouse-like marsupial.

Are possums the same as opossums? Good question. **Opossums** are the group of American marsupials that are in the family Didelphideae. According to one source, it is derived from a Native American word, "wapathemwa."

Possums, on the other hand, are Australasian animals that come from several different marsupial families. Australians named these animals "possums" because they looked so much like the American opossums, even though the two groups have no close scientific relationship beyond being marsupials. If this isn't confusing enough, people sometimes call the Virginia opossum a "possum."

The whole possum/opossum problem illustrates why it's important to have scientific names for animals and not only the common names that we use in everyday speech.

The Virginia **opossum** is found in North America.

The brush-tail **possum** is found in Australia.

Short and Sweet

Millions of acres of southwest Australia are covered by stunning flowering plants belonging to the genus *Banksia* (BANK-see-uh). These flowers are not pollinated by birds, bees, butterflies, or even bats. Amazingly, they are pollinated by a tiny marsupial called the honey possum.

Honey possums feed almost solely on nectar and pollen from flowers. These miniature marsupials are about the length of a small mouse and weigh only about as much as two nickels. They nimbly climb up onto the *Banksia* plants and feed by sticking their long tongues into the flowers. A honey possum can eat its weight in nectar every day.

Female possums grow almost twice as large as males and tend to live in smaller areas with lots of flowers. Males scramble more widely to find food and females to mate with. The possum mom has between one and four young at a time. Because the female mates with many males, each baby in a litter may have a different father.

Baby honey possums stay in their mother's pouch for about two months. About three months later, they are ready to breed. A female can bear two litters a year, which is important because few honey possums live past their first year. Their lives are short, but very sweet.

The honey possum has a long tongue that is perfect for getting nectar from a *Banksia*.

THE "SKUNK POSSUM"

People have often compared the striped possum, *Dactylpsila trivirgata* (dak-tilp-SIL-uh tri ver-GAW-tuh) to a skunk. Its bold black-and-white stripes are partly to blame, but so is the animal's ability to emit a powerful odor.

Early scientists weren't too impressed by these smelly animals. One observer called the striped possum "a rather stupid creature." Recent researchers, though, have revealed that striped possums are wonderfully adapted to their way of life.

Striped possums live in the rainforests of Australia and New Guinea. Two biologists, Dr. D.R. Rawlins and K.A. Handasyde, discovered that striped possums eat mostly insects—especially insects that bore into the trunks of trees and rotten logs.

The possums crawl all over tree trunks tapping the bark with their forefeet, much as a woodpecker does with its beak. The changing sound of the tapping probably alerts the striped possum where a tasty beetle or fat grub is hiding inside the wood. Once it has located its prey, the striped possum tears away at the bark with its powerful lower incisors.

Two additional features help the possum to snag its snack. One is a very long tongue. The other is an especially long fourth finger that it uses to probe into tiny holes and "hook out" its prey.

The striped possum (*left*) and common skunk (*right*) share similar coloration. But the skunk is *not* a marsupial.

POSSUM PROBLEMS

In the year 1837 or so, some people in New Zealand got a bright idea. "Let's introduce a new fur-bearing critter from Australia to build up a fur industry," they told each other. The animal they chose was another marsupial: *Trichosurus vulpecula* (tri-ko-SOOR-us vul-PEK-u-la), the common brush-tail possum.

It was a big mistake.

In contrast to other phalangerids, the common brush-tail possum is one of the world's best-studied marsupials, both because of its pest status and its commercial use. In its native Australia, the brush-tail possum fits in well with the rest of the ecosystem. It eats the leaves of eucalyptus and beech trees along with assorted fruits, buds, bark, and other plant materials. In turn, it is preyed on by dingoes, owls, Tasmanian devils, cats, dogs, monitor lizards, and snakes. However, many New Zealanders consider the brush-tail possum Public Enemy Number One.

Ian Bradley works for New Zealand's Department of Conservation. "Possums are a pest of plague proportions," he explains. "Every night an estimated seventy million possums chew their way through twenty-one thousand

a common brush-tail possum with its baby

metric tonnes (more than forty-six million pounds) of native forest. That's the equivalent of one hundred ninety *million* hamburgers each night. Although they eat a variety of foods, possums frequently browse a particular tree, stripping it in a few nights and eventually killing the tree."

In some places, possums have devoured entire forest canopies, endangering many of the country's native plant and animal species. But the possum hasn't stopped there. It eats the eggs and chicks of many native birds and has developed a fondness for New Zealand's rare giant land snails. "They can also be a carrier and transmitter of the disease bovine (cow) tuberculosis," Ian Bradley explains. "This threatens New Zealand's beef and venison exports."

Why has this possum become such a problem? One reason is that New Zealand has very few predators for the invading marsupials to contend with. Another reason is that the possums find many of New Zealand's plants much tastier than the plants back home in Australia. "They are also thrifty eaters," Ian Bradley adds. "Like many other Australian marsupials, they can maintain themselves on thirty percent less food than a rabbit or a rat or a sheep. Hence they can survive on poor and irregular food supplies."

"Because we cannot get rid of possums, we try to control them," Ian Bradley says. For years, New Zealand offered bounties on the possums while hunters also killed them for their fur. Now, all-out war has been declared. Poison, traps, and even parasites and diseases are being used to fight back this marauding marsupial. The result? The common brush-tail possum is still going strong.

The common brush-tail possum has become a major pest in New Zealand.

GREAT GLIDERS!

Of all of Australasia's possums, none are more astonishing than those that glide. At least seven species of possums have evolved to be able to glide, including the sugar gliders that are now popular as pets in North America. How do they do it? With the help of a membrane called a *patagium* (pa-ta-JEE-um). This special patch of skin extends from the possums' wrists to their ankles. When the possums are at rest or scurrying about, the patagium just looks like a bit of loose, wrinkled skin. When a possum leaps out from a tree, the patagium spreads into an elegant airfoil.

With their patagiums, some gliders can glide more than one hundred yards between trees. Using its tail and feet as rudders, a glider can adjust its flight and even make a U-turn!

As you might expect, gliders are especially adapted to live in tall, mature forests. They eat

When the sugar glider is not gliding, its "wings" are loose skin.

a variety of foods: sap, flowers, insects, spiders, and other small prey. Being able to glide helps keep them safe from foxes and other ground predators as they cruise from tree to tree.

Eutherian mammals called "flying squirrels" have also evolved to glide. Like the gliding possums, flying squirrels have a patagium that can be stretched out into an airfoil. However, these two groups of animals evolved independently.

High Society

Marsupials aren't known for being very sociable. Sure, a few kangaroos hang out in mobs, but most marsupials want little to do with each other. Not so with gliders. All but one glider species, the greater glider, form family groups of between two and ten adults. As they glide through the forest, they loudly call to each other to stay in touch.

THE MARSUPIAL SLOTHS: CUSCUSES AND MORE!

The family Phalangeridae (fa-lan-JER-i-dee) has between seventeen and twenty-two species, with names like cuscus (koos-koos), brush-tail possum, and scaly-tailed possum. The phalangerids are the most widespread family of Australian marsupials. They range through Australia, New Guinea, and many islands of eastern Indonesia.

Phalangerids are beautiful animals, known for their thick fur and strange, bulging eyes. They can be thought of as Australasia's "sloths," because they move slowly through treetops, where they eat mostly tender, young leaves. Their prehensile tails help them feel secure far above the forest floor.

Scientists know little about most of these species, but in the late 1990s, a group of researchers spent several months observing the world's largest phalangerid, an animal called the bear cuscus, *Ailurops ursinus* (A-lur-ops ur-SINE-us). The bear cuscus lives on the Indonesian island of Sulawesi, as well as on several nearby islands. A handsome animal that can weigh up to twenty-two pounds, this species often forms male-female pairs—an unusual lifestyle for a marsupial, since most marsupial pairs have little to do with each other after mating.

The researchers discovered that bear cuscuses spend only a little more than an hour a day eating. They spend about *two-thirds* of their time sleeping or resting. Why? The same old marsupial story—it takes a lot of time and energy for the bear cuscus to digest the leaves that it eats. These leaves are high in fiber and poor in nutrition. Like the koala and wombat, the bear cuscus has special digestive features that allow it to process this challenging food. Even so, digestion is an energy-intensive project—the perfect excuse to pack in a lot of Zs.

a bear cuscus (*Ailurops ursinus*)

a spotted cuscus (*Spilocuscus maculatus*)

OF BANDICOOTS, BILBIES, NUMBATS, AND MOLES

It's a rat. No, a rabbit. Ah, it's a mini-kangaroo. No, looks more like a . . . what *is* that critter? If you're in Australia or New Guinea and you just don't know, chances are you're looking at a bandicoot.

About twenty-two species of these smallish, sort-of cute, active little marsupials live in Australasia. They range in size from about half a pound to more than ten pounds. They live in almost all habitats, where they ravenously feast on earthworms, fungi, spiders, insects, plant tubers, fruit, and grubs—with snails, lizards, and mice thrown in for dessert.

Bandicoots are solitary, nocturnal animals. Often, they don't seem to like each other. At a site in western Australia, biologists reintroduced western barred bandicoots to a place they hadn't lived in decades. When the scientists went out to see how the bandicoots were doing, they discovered that most of the animals had patches of fur missing from their rumps and had lost parts of their tails. The scientists concluded that the bandicoots had inflicted these injuries on each other, probably in fights over territories or mates.

an eastern barred bandicoot

48

SPEED MATING

Speaking of mates, bandicoots hold the record for fast births. Bandicoot babies are born only about twelve days after the female mates. This is the shortest gestation recorded for any mammal. After they are born, baby bandicoots stay in their mom's pouch for about fifty days. As soon as one litter is weaned, another is born. With such a speedy turnaround, a female can bear up to four litters each mating season.

Bandicoots are the only marsupials known to develop a *placenta* during pregnancy. A placenta is an organ that passes important nutrition from the mother to developing embryos. Eutherian mammals like humans and whales always develop placentas, but most marsupials do not. Having a placenta, though, may help bandicoots breed more quickly than other marsupials. It also raises a question: If bandicoots have a placenta, are they closely related to eutherian mammals? The answer is no. The placenta in bandicoots evolved separately from the placenta in humans and other eutherian mammals.

Having a placenta also doesn't mean that bandicoots are especially good parents. As soon as baby bandicoots are weaned, they are on their own as the mother turns her attention to her next litter.

A baby bandicoot eats from a spoon.

RABBIT EARS

In dry, sandy regions of Australia lives a particularly strange-looking bandicoot. It's called a rabbit-eared bandicoot, or bilby. Bilbies have oversized "rabbit ears," especially long hind feet, and beautiful long tails. With their strong front legs and sharp claws, bilbies dig networks of burrows in the sandy soil and may regularly use up to two dozen burrows at a time.

A bilby's long, pointed nose detects a wide variety of bulbs, spiders, grubs, ants, and other tasty treats. Its large ears pick up the tiniest sounds. It's a good thing, too. For thousands of years, bilbies were a favorite food of aboriginal Australians. More recently, bilbies have had to watch out for introduced predators, such as foxes and cats.

a rabbit-eared bandicoot, or bilby

Make Way for the Easter Bilby

Once common throughout most of Australia, bilbies now live in only a few areas and are considered endangered. To help raise money to protect bilbies, an Australian retail chain began making chocolate Easter bilbies. A nationwide campaign urged Australians to switch from buying chocolate Easter bunnies to buying Easter bilbies instead. The manufacturer donates profits from the sale to the Save the Bilby Fund. Since 1994, Easter bilby sales have raised tens of thousands of dollars to protect this unique, big-eared animal.

TROUBLE WITH TERMITES? CALL N-U-M-B-A-T!

If you saw someone you didn't like out on the schoolyard, you might be tempted to shout "Hey, numbat!" Careful, though. You might be paying the person a compliment.

Numbats are, in fact, one of Australia's most beautiful and interesting marsupials. About the size of a large squirrel, the numbat is one of the few marsupials that is mostly active during the daytime. You might see one in the open woodlands of western Australia, tearing into hard soil and rotten logs. What is it looking for? Termites, of course!

Numbats—also called "banded anteaters"—have evolved a special fondness for termites and ants. Their strong forearms, sturdy claws, and sharp teeth allow the numbats to pursue their prey by ripping open the insects' nests.

However, it's the long, tube-shaped tongue that really allows a numbat to slurp up social insects on a large scale. The tongue is about four inches long and has been known to snag up to twenty *thousand* termites in a single day! A special hard palate in the numbat's mouth helps crush the tough exoskeletons of the insects.

Like most other marsupials, numbats are solitary animals. After a hard day slurping down termite shakes, they hole up in hollow logs. A mother numbat has a litter of two to four babies between January and March. She digs a short underground burrow that leads to a leaf- or grass-lined nest. When the babies are a little older, mom leaves them in the nest while she goes out stalking her distinctive diet.

The numbat uses its long tongue to catch termites and ants.

In the Dirt Down Under: Marsupial Moles

You're probably getting the idea that marsupials have evolved to live in almost every kind of habitat—woodlands, rocky outcrops, rainforests, you name it. In the harsh, sandy deserts of central Australia, one four-inch-long marsupial has even ventured underground. Its aboriginal name is the *itjaritjari*. Others call it the marsupial mole.

The marsupial mole hunts underground insects and other invertebrates. It is ideally adapted to a *subterranean*, or underground, existence. For digging through the soil, it has sturdy, shovel-shaped front claws and a hard plate for a nose. It is also completely blind, having long ago lost the need for functional eyes. It does have holes for ears, which are probably adapted for hearing underground.

Since their discovery by Europeans in the late 1800s, the moles have remained largely a mystery. Few were ever seen, and almost nothing was known about their habits. Recently, however, scientists have teamed up with Australian aboriginal people to locate and learn more about the moles. The team has dispelled at least one marsupial mole myth. For more than a century, people thought the moles "swam" through the sand, leaving behind no permanent tunnels. However, the scientist-aboriginal team learned that the moles actually dig vast, permanent systems of underground tunnels.

The team hopes to learn a lot more about the moles. One big question is "how many moles are there?" To help find out, scientists are installing underground listening devices called "geophones." With luck, these geophones will be able to distinguish between different moles as they crawl through their tunnels. They may also teach us a lot about mole behavior, bringing many more marsupial mole mysteries to the surface.

This marsupial mole is munching on a centipede.

MARSUPIAL MEAT-EATERS: TASMANIAN DEVILS, QUOLLS, AND MORE

After reading about other marsupials, you might be asking yourself, "Are there any real meat-eaters in the bunch?" The answer to that question is yes. Take a look at these meat-eaters of the family Dasyuridae (das-ee-UR-i-dee).

The dasyurids include at least sixty-two species from Australia, New Guinea, and nearby islands. Most dasyurids are small, extremely active, shrew- or rat-like animals. They pounce on any prey they can kill—from insects to lizards, birds, and small mammals. Dasyurids include a wide variety of marsupial "mice," as well as dunnarts, ningauis, kultarrs, kowaris, and mulgaras. Despite their small sizes, most dasyurids carry their babies in pouches. The males of many dasyruid species live less than one year and die shortly after mating.

The largest dasyurid, though, lives much longer. It happens to be one of Australia's most famous marsupials, the Tasmanian devil. And a cat-sized dasyurid, the quoll, lives about five to six years.

The Tasmanian devil is one of Australia's most popular creatures.

The quoll is about the size of a cat.

Meat-Eating Marsupials

The **mulgara** looks a lot like a quoll and is a formidable desert predator. It has a special fondness for mice, devouring them from head to tail while peeling their skins inside out.

mulgara

Dunnarts—also called "narrow-footed marsupial mice"—are little bundles of energy three to five inches long, not including their long tails. There are more than twenty species and almost all are nocturnal. At top speed, they bound forward on their slender hind feet.

dunnart

The size of a large rat, the **kowari** avidly hunts insects, spiders, birds, rodents, and lizards. Its beautiful furry tail would make a great duster!

Ningauis are even smaller than dunnarts. Several could fit into your hand at once. When temperatures plunge or there isn't enough food, they sink into a daily *torpor*—a kind of temporary hibernation.

ningauis

The **kultarr** lives in dry savannahs, grasslands, and deserts. It nests in logs and may also use the burrows of other animals. Its body is three to four inches long.

kultarr

FROM REAL LIFE TO THE BIG SCREEN

Millions of people grew up watching cartoons showing fierce, man-sized Tasmanian devils whirling across the landscape like tornadoes, kicking up dust and terrorizing everyone. Most of us are surprised to learn two things. First, there really are Tasmanian devils. Second, real Tasmanian devils are not only much smaller than their cartoon counterparts, but they aren't nearly as ornery.

"When they are in contact with another devil," explains Tasmanian devil expert Elaine Kirchner, "there is a lot of ritualized fighting. It appears they're going to tear each other to pieces, but that's just their social structure. If they're at a carcass, the dominant devil's going to get there first, and he's going to say, 'No, let me have the part that I want.'"

Unlike cartoon devils, real Tasmanian devils are only about the size of a small dog. At times, they even appear slow and clumsy. They hunt at night with their noses to the ground, sniffing for a variety of small prey. They've been known to eat wallabies, wombats, and rabbits. In the past, the animals also were thought to prey on sheep, but this is probably rare. "They're more scavengers than they are predators," Elaine Kirchner explains. "They really would prefer to eat something that's already cold and smelly and dead."

(*above*) A full-grown Tasmanian devil is the size of a small dog. (*right*) Tasmania is an island-state of Australia.

DEVILS AT HOME

Tasmanian devils once lived on Australia's mainland but were probably driven out by Australia's wild dogs, or *dingoes*, which appeared on the continent about five thousand years ago. Today, the island of Tasmania is the sole home of the Tasmanian devils.

During the day, they sleep in nests of leaves or bark in caves, hollow logs, wombat holes, or dense bushes. "They're very solitary animals," explains Elaine Kirchner. "They don't live in a family group unless the mother is raising young. The female is dominant nearly the entire year with the exception of the few days when she's mating. Then, the male dominates the female. After that's over, she runs him off and wants nothing to do with him."

The female has three or four babies—very *cute* babies. These babies spend about three and a half months in Mom's backward-facing pouch and are totally weaned after about eight months.

 ## Devils with Personality

One thing that real Tasmanian devils share with their cartoon counterparts is personality. In the Fort Wayne (Indiana) Zoo, Elaine Kirchner describes some of the little devils she's been around, "Some of them were grumpy and just wanted everyone to leave them alone. Some were just kind of laid-back and would watch you when you were in the area, but they knew the habits of the keepers. If they heard us coming, they assumed food was involved. Their only happiness was food. They're very, *very* food-driven."

A young Tasmanian devil learns to scavenge for food.

Quolls: Australiasia's "Native Cats"

Some of the most beautiful marsupials anywhere are quolls, or "native cats." Quolls are about the size of rabbits but are still considered some of Australasia's largest marsupial carnivores. Six species live in New Guinea and Australia. Their striking white spots remind one of a little leopard or jaguar.

Quolls feast on insects, but larger quolls will attack wallabies and poultry. "They're exceptionally fast-moving," says Elaine Kirchner. "They like to climb up trees and on ledges and places like that. One of the reasons the devils and quolls can co-exist in Tasmania is because they're operating in different niches within the ecosystem. They'll go up and raid birds' nests, whereas the devils are on the ground."

Quolls have large territories, up to a couple of square miles. Often, males outnumber females so, not surprisingly, females often breed with more than one male. Quolls give birth to large litters of up to sixteen or seventeen babies, but the mother only has eight teats, so many of the newborns die.

A mother quoll takes her babies for a night-time walk.

EXTINCT AND ENDANGERED: MARSUPIALS IN TROUBLE

Looking at the success of the Virginia opossum in North America, you might think that marsupials are doing quite well in the world. And it's true that some marsupials are thriving. Many others, however, are in serious trouble.

In North and South America, the destruction of rainforests and other habitats threatens many marsupials. In Australasia, marsupials face their biggest challenges.

THE THYLACINE: "TASMANIAN TIGER"

In 1936, a remarkable animal died in a zoo in Hobart, Tasmania. Three feet long and standing about two feet high, the animal had bold tiger stripes along its back, rump, and very long tail. While it was alive, the animal walked or trotted in a way that could be mistaken for a wolf or coyote. But this animal was no canid. It was a predatory marsupial called a thylacine (THY-la-seen). And it was the last known survivor of its species.

The thylacine was also called the Tasmanian wolf or Tasmanian tiger. That's no coincidence. Like many other marsupials, the thylacine presents an astonishing case of *convergent evolution*—the evolution of similar features in distant, unrelated species. Over millions of years, the thylacine evolved many of the same features as the dog family on other continents. It

an artist's rendition of a thylacine

58

ran on four legs. Its teeth were well suited for subduing large prey. It even had the compact body-shape of dogs.

The thylacine was just as successful as dogs, too. While wolves, dogs, and coyotes flourished on other continents, the thylacine became the top hunter throughout New Guinea and Australia. It fed on wallabies, kangaroos, and other large marsupial prey. When aboriginal people brought dingoes to Australia, however, thylacines began losing ground. Members of the dog family, dingoes proved to be superior hunters to thylacines. People hunting for game may also have reduced the amount of food for these native predators. By about three thousand years ago, these two factors drove thylacines from the Australian mainland.

This is a photo of one of the last surviving thylacines. They are now extinct.

EUROPEAN INVASION

But the thylacine still survived on the large dingo-free island of Tasmania. Here, there were plenty of animals to eat, including wallabies, potoroos, and bettongs. In the early 1800s, though, Europeans arrived in Australia and quickly settled in Tasmania. These humans began clearing forests and raising domestic sheep. The sheep became easy prey for the thylacine.

By the 1830s, farmers and ranchers began targeting the thylacine as a nuisance animal. Bounties were offered on it. People began a widespread campaign to shoot, trap, and poison the animals. The clearing of woodlands, the introduction of domestic dogs, and disease also took their toll. The last known wild thylacine was killed in 1930. The last living thylacine died in the Hobart Zoo in 1936.

Unfortunately for marsupials, the loss of the thylacine was just a taste of things to come.

GAINS AND LOSSES

The arrival of humans, especially Europeans, to Australia has actually benefited some marsupials. A few large, grain-eating macropods, such as red and gray kangaroos, have thrived as Australia's landscape has been converted to farms and grazing lands. Today there are so many eastern and western gray kangaroos, red kangaroos, and wallaroos that some Australians consider them pests. People hunt these large animals for their meat and skins and to control their numbers. Other marsupials, such as the brush-tail possum, have benefited by being introduced to new areas where they have no competition.

Unfortunately, a vast number of marsupial species have suffered at the hands of human beings. Some, such as the thylacine, have been directly persecuted by people. For most, however, it has been other actions that have created marsupial mayhem.

Australia is a vast area of farms and grazing lands.

OF RABBITS, RED FOXES, AND TOADS

As people have colonized the globe, we've had a tendency to bring along familiar and useful species with us. But when these species are released into new environments, they can quickly create unnatural nightmares. Hordes of introduced rabbits, for example, have devastated wildlands throughout Australia. They have devoured millions of acres of farm and grazing lands and have destroyed the habitat of many native marsupials.

Red foxes and feral (untamed) cats have created an even greater calamity. Bandicoots, bilbies, numbats, and dozens of other smaller marsupials provide ideal prey for these two introduced predators. According to Australian scientist Jeff Short, "Eighteen species have become extinct and twenty-six species have suffered severe range contraction in the two hundred and ten years since European settlement."

Many of these declines are a direct result of red foxes and cats, neither of which has any significant natural enemies in Australia.

Even supposedly helpful introductions of exotic animals can have devastating effects on native animals. The cane toad was originally released in Australia to control two harmful beetle pests that were damaging the sugar cane crop. Unfortunately, the giant amphibian turned out to be toxic to a wide variety of other animals. When bitten, the toads release a lethal secretion from their poison glands, and more often than not, the toad's attacker drops dead. Quolls have been especially hard hit by this situation. Wherever the cane toad has spread in tropical Australia, native quolls have disappeared. To add insult to injury, the cane toad turned out to do nothing to control the beetle pests they were brought in to eat!

feral cat

red fox

cane toad

AN UNEASY EXISTENCE

Millions of koalas used to live in Australia. However, their habits and fine fur have led to a precarious existence. In the early part of the twentieth century, hunters killed more than three million of the animals for their pelts. Since then, widespread clearing of eucalyptus forests has drastically reduced their range. "Habitat loss, without a doubt, is the greatest threat to koalas," David Dique explains. "In urbanized areas, cars and domestic dogs also pose big problems."

Since koalas live in trees, it's not easy to tell exactly how their populations are doing. "In Queensland," Dr. Dique says, "our best guess is that we have one hundred thousand to three hundred thousand koalas left. In New South Wales, there is probably a minimum of fifty thousand. And in Victoria and South Australia combined, there are several hundred thousand. But it's difficult to say for sure."

An example of deforestation in Australia shows a loss of several eucalyptus trees.

OTHER PROBLEMS

As if hunting, habitat destruction, predation, and poisoning weren't enough, diseases seem to be taking a new toll on some Australasian species, too. A disease called chlamydia swept through koala populations in the late 1980s and early 1990s. The disease not only makes many female koalas unable to reproduce, but it also causes blindness in both males and females. In some areas, chlamydia has severely reduced or even eliminated koala populations.

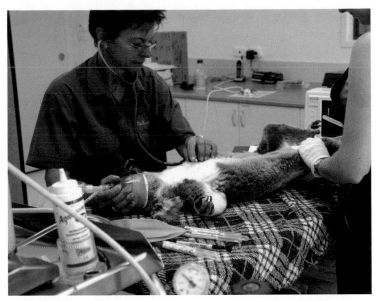
A careperson treats a sick koala.

a mom and baby Tasmanian devils

More recently, DFTD—Devil Facial Tumor Disease—has attacked Tasmanian devils. According to Australia's Department of the Environment and Heritage, "The cancers begin as small lesions or lumps in and around the mouth and quickly develop into large tumors on the face, neck, and shoulders." These tumors quickly prevent the devils from eating, and the animals starve to death within months of getting the disease.

Additional problems for marsupials include deaths by automobiles and even global warming, which promises to alter many of the habitats where marsupials live. Faced with so many threats, the question for Australasia's marsupials might be: "Is there any *good* news?"

HARD WORK AND HOPE: MARSUPIAL CONSERVATION

Nearly half of Australasia's marsupials face the possibility of going extinct in the near future. However, people are steadily fighting back to save these animals. Approaches to saving marsupials vary. For instance, scientists have moved endangered northern quolls to offshore islands that are not infested with cane toads. They hope that when the cane toad problem is solved or improved, quolls can be returned to the mainland.

Back in 1991, when the population of eastern barred bandicoots dropped to about one hundred survivors, scientists began a captive breeding program. After they had built up the

Reducing Traffic Tolls on Quolls

Automobiles take a huge toll on Australian marsupials. Thousands of koalas, kangaroos, and other marsupials are run down on the nation's roads. In Tasmania's Cradle Mountain-Lake St. Clair National Park, the improvement of one road led to higher vehicle speeds—and a huge increase in traffic deaths of marsupials. In a span of just seventeen months, the entire population of eastern quolls and half of the Tasmanian devils were wiped out. However, the park quickly implemented measures to slow traffic and increase driver awareness. Within two years, both quoll and Tasmanian devil populations rebounded. This shows that, with a little care and planning, marsupials can be protected.

bandicoot population, researchers began releasing the animals back into wild, protected habitats.

In New Guinea, tree kangaroos are a favorite source of meat for people. But as the human population has increased, overhunting has severely reduced the numbers of tree kangaroos. This is a significant problem for these animals because they are very slow to reproduce.

Lisa Dabek of Seattle's Woodland Park Zoo has been working closely with people in New Guinea to protect the tree kangaroos. "I've worked with this same community for about ten years," Dr. Dabek explains, "and they have agreed to set aside portions of their hunting lands so that there are safe places for the tree kangaroos to live and breed. We describe it as a wildlife bank. If you have safe areas where animals can breed, then their offspring can disperse into the hunting grounds where people can hunt them. Also, tree kangaroos aren't the only marsupials that live in these forests. The safe area is also protecting a lot of other marsupials, including pademelons, forest wallabies, and bandicoots."

Tree kangaroos are a source of meat for some people in New Guinea.

The pademelon is now extinct on mainland Australia. It can only be found in Tasmania.

THE BIG PICTURE

There is no simple solution to saving marsupials. Protecting each species will take learning about the needs of and threats to that particular species. Certainly, controlling introduced species such as foxes, cats, and cane toads will be a key to saving many marsupials. Preventing the destruction of forests and other habitats will also be critical.

What humans do on a global scale also matters. Global warming poses perhaps the biggest threat to species everywhere on the planet. Global warming is caused by certain gases, known as *greenhouse gases*, in Earth's atmosphere. These gases—especially carbon dioxide—prevent the sun's rays from being reflected back into space. Instead, they are trapped and raise global temperatures.

Humans generate enormous quantities of greenhouse gases through our activities—especially burning fossil fuels. Most of the electricity we use is generated by burning coal and oil, while our automobiles are powered directly by the combustion of gasoline. The carbon dioxide generated by these activities is raising global temperatures and destroying habitats on an unprecedented scale. Already, warmer global temperatures are melting polar ice sheets, killing coral reefs, and reducing rainfall in many areas. Scientists believe that over the next century, many forests will become grasslands, while many grasslands will become deserts. As these habitats disappear, so will the animals that live in them.

Humans and nature can coexist in ways that benefit both.

WHAT CAN YOU DO?

If we truly care about marsupials and other species, we each need to recognize how, even thousands of miles away, we can contribute to their survival. Get involved. Practice energy conservation in your own home. Urge government leaders to invest more money and planning in alternative energy, mass transit, conservation, and the control of invasive species. Your actions will make a difference and are the best chance of survival, not only for marsupials, but also for millions of Earth's of other species.

a koala

a quokka

a sugar glider

ACKNOWLEDGMENTS

The topic of marsupials is large and complex, and I could not have attempted writing this book without the help of many people. I would first like to thank Dr. Ron Pine at the University of Kansas Museum of Natural History for his extensive help shepherding me through New World marsupials. Dr. Pine's expertise and review of my manuscript are largely responsible for my being able to present these fascinating, little-known animals in a way that does them justice.

I also greatly appreciate the insights on the Virginia opossum from Alice Seyfried, Curator at the St. Louis Zoo. Alice also helped me with that popular group of Australian marsupials, the macropods, as did two other wonderful experts: Adrienne Miller, Marsupial Registrar at the Audubon Zoo; and Dr. Lisa Dabek, Director of Conservation at Seattle's Woodland Park Zoo.

For wombats and Tasmanian devils, I was grateful to receive the hands-on wisdom and knowledge of Elaine Kirchner, the Area Manager for the Australia exhibit at Indiana's Fort Wayne Children's Zoo. Dr. David Dique, Principal Conservation Officer for Queensland's (Australia) Environmental Protection Agency, provided me with invaluable information and perspective on koalas. I also would like to thank Ian Bradley of New Zealand's Department of Conservation for describing the impact of the common brush-tail possum.

Lastly, I would like to thank my editor Tanya Dean for suggesting this project and for putting it all together. Thank you, everyone!

FOR FURTHER READING

BOOKS

Few recent, up-to-date books about marsupials have been published for older readers. Most of those that are available are series books with the exception of the first book below. Here are a few titles to get started.

Quest for the Tree Kangaroos: An Expedition to The Cloud Forest of New Guinea by Sy Montgomery and Nic Bishop. Houghton Mifflin Co., 2006.
A wonderful book focusing on the work of Lisa Dabek to learn about and save tree kangaroos. Read this!

Meateating Marsupials by Erin Pembrey Swan. Scholastic Library Publishing, 2002.
This series book focuses on marsupial carnivores.

Kangaroos and Other Marsupials, Vol. 6 by Julie A. Fenton and World Book, Inc. Staff (Editor). World Book Inc., 2002.
A series book that discusses marsupials.

Pocket Babies by Katherine McGlade Marko. Scholastic Library Publishing, 1995.
Another series book about marsupials.

WEB SITES

For marsupials, Web sites are (in general) a better bet than books for learning about marsupials—with the exception of this book, of course! Many Web sites are available. Here are some that I particularly like.

Australian Museum site on Riversleigh
http://www.amonline.net.au/fossil_sites/riversleigh.htm
This site discusses the remarkable fossil finds of ancient marsupials and other fossils discovered at the Riversleigh World Heritage Site. The Australian Museum site has a lot of other interesting information about Australian animals, as well.

Australiafauna.com
http://www.australianfauna.com/
This great site focuses on a wide range of Australian animals including koalas, wombats, and kangaroos.

The National Opossum Society
http://www.opossum.org/
The site is dedicated to education about and protection of our own native marsupial, the Virginia opossum.

New Zealand Department of Conservation
http://www.doc.govt.nz/templates/podcover.aspx?id=33422
This site explains and explores the brush-tail possum problem in New Zealand.

Australian Koala Foundation
http://www.doc.govt.nz/templates/podcover.aspx?id=33422
On this site, you will find interesting information on koalas and their conservation.

 # BIBLIOGRAPHY

BOOKS AND BOOK CHAPTERS

Allegre, Claude. *The Behavior of the Earth*. Cambridge, MA: Harvard University Press, 1988.

Archer, Michael and John Kirsch. "The evolution and classification of marsupials." *Marsupials*. Cambridge University Press, 2006.

Eisenberg, John F. *Mammals of the Neotropics*, Volume 1: *The Northern Neotropics. Chicago*: University of Chicago Press, 1989.

Halls, Kelly Milner. *Wild Dogs: Past and Present*. Plain City, OH: Darby Creek Pub, 2005.

Hunsaker, Don, Editor. *The Biology of Marsupials*. New York: Academic Press, 1977.

Kirsch, John. "The Classification of Marsupials." In *The Biology of Marsupials*. Academic Press, New York, 1977.

McKay, G.M. and J.W. Winter. "26. Phalangeridae." *Fauna of Australia*.

Nowak, Ronald M. *Walker's Marsupials of the World*. Baltimore: Johns Hopkins University Press, 2005.

Price, A. Grenfell, Editor. *The Explorations of Captain James Cook in the Pacific*. New York: Dover Publishing, 1971.

Strahan, R., editor. *Mammals of Australia*. Washington, D.C.: Smithsonian Inst. Press, 1995.

PAPERS

Belcher, C.A. "Demographics of tiger quoll (*Dasyurus maculatus maculatus*) populations in south–eastern Australia. *Australia Journal of Zoology*. Vol. 51, pp. 611–626, 2003.

"The faster a 'roo' travels, the more energy it saves." *Smithsonian*. V. 24, no. 8, pp. 102–117, November 1993.

Dennis, Andrew J. "Marsupial Gardeners." *Nature Australia*. Vol. 28 (No. 1), pp. 26–33, Winter 2004.

Dennis, Carina. "A mole in hand…" *Nature*. Vol. 432, November 11, 2004.

Domico, Terry. "The Red Meat That's Good for You." *Natural History*. Vol. 109, No. 2, p. 37, March 2000.

Dwiyahreni, Asri A., et. al. "Diet and Activity of the Bear Cuscus, *Ailurops ursinus*, in North Sulawesi, Indonesia." *Journal of Mammalogy*. Vol. 80, No. 3, pp. 905–912, August 1999.

Eliot, John L. "Revenge of the cane toads: alien amphibian bites back at Australian quolls." *National Geographic*. Vol. 207, No. 3, March 2005.

EPBC Act Policy Statement 3.6: Nationally Threatened Species and Ecological Communities: Tasmanian Devil (*Sarcophilus harrisii*). Australian Government, Department of the Environment and Heritage, July 2006.

Garland, Lachlan. "Speed kills animals too." *Ecos*. July–September 2000.

Kimble, Daniel P. "Didelphid Behavior." *Neuroscience and Biobehavioral Reviews*. Vol. 21, No. 3, pp. 361–399, 1997.

Luo, Zhe–Xi, et. al. "An Early Cretaceous Tribosphenic Mammal and Metatherian Evolution." *Science*. Vol. 302, pp. 1934–1940, December 12, 2003.

Mize, Jim. "Why Opossum Starts With 'O'." *South Carolina Wildlife*. March–April 2005.

Moore, Benjamin D. and William J. Foley. "A review of feeding and diet selection in koalas (*Phascolarctos cinereus*)." *Australia Journal of Zoology*. Vol. 48, pp. 317–333, 2000.

Nelson, John E. and Robert T. Gemmell. "Birth in the northern quoll, *Dasyurus hallucatus* (Marsupialia: Dasyuridae)." *Australia Journal of Zoology*. Vol. 51, pp. 187–198, 2003.

Ogburn, Sarah and Linda Brogdon. "Natural History of the Grey Short–Tailed Opossum (*Monodelphis domestica*). On www.baa.duke.edu/companat/BAA_289L_2004/Natural_History/Opossum/opossum_natural_history.htm

Paddock, Richard C. "A Vexing, Virulent Varmint." *L.A. Times*. May 25, 2001.

Pyper, Wendy. "Koalas are losing out to traffic." *Ecos*. Issue 118, p. 31, January–March 2004.

Rand, Austin Loomer. "Some original observations on the habits of Dactylopsila trivirgata Gray." *American Museum Novitiates*. No. 957. 1937.

Rankmore, Brooke. "Quolls get the jump on cane toads." *Australian Geographic*. Issue 80, p. 26, October–December 2005.

Rawlins, D.R. AND K.A. Handasyde. "The feeding ecology of the striped possum *Dactylopsila trivirgata* (Marsupialia: Petauridae) in far north Queensland, Australia. *Journal of Zoology*. Vol. 257, pp. 195–206, London, 2002.

Richards, J.D. and Jeff Short. "Reintroduction and establishment of the western barred bandicoot *Perameles bougainville* (Marsupialia: Peramelidae) at Shark Bay, Western Australia. *Biological Conservation*. Vol. 109, pp. 181–195, 2003.

Szabo, Michael. "Australia's Marsupials—Going, Going, Gone?" *New Scientist*. pp. 30–35, January 28, 1995.

Short, Jeff. "The extinction of rat–kangaroos (Marsupialia: Potoroidae) in New South Wales, Australia. *Biological Conservation*. Vol. 86, No. 3, pp. 365–377, December 1998.

Springer, Mark S. et al. "The origin of the Australasian marsupial fauna and the phylogenetic affinities of the enigmatic monito del monte and marsupial mole." *Proceedings of the Royal Society of London*. Vol. 265, pp. 2381–2386, 1998.

Thwaites, Tim et al. "Everything you always wanted to know about kangaroos." *International Wildlife*. Vol. 27, No. 5, pp. 34–44, September–October 1997.

Wooller, R.D. et al. "Opportunistic breeding in the polyandrous honey possum, *Tarsipes rostratus*. *Australia Journal of Zoology*. Vol. 48, pp. 669–680, 2000.

WEB SITES

http://animaldiversity.ummz.umich.edu/site/accounts/information/Metatheria.html

www.riversleigh.qld.gov.au

http://byunews.byu.edu/release.aspx?story=archive04/Jul/isthmus

http://gsa.confex.com/gsa/2003CD/finalprogram/abstract_52136.htm

www.knowyoursto.com/didelphidae/chironectes.html

www.nsrl.ttu.edu/tmot1/didevirg.htm

www.wombania.com

http://museum.nhm.uga.edu/gawildlife/mammals/marsupialia/didelphimorphia/dvirginiana.html

www.fastload.org/co/Colocolo.html

www.landcareresearch.co.nz/news/release.asp?Ne_ID=76

www.doc.govt.nz/Conservation/002~Animal–Pests/Possums/index.asp

www.deh.gov.au/biodiversity/trade–use/wild–harvest/possum/possm01.html

www.bbc.co.uk/nature/wildfacts/factfiles/943.shtml

www.bbc.co.uk/nature/wildfacts/factfiles/655.shtml

www.abc.net.au/quantum/s244451.htm#transcript

www.nationalparks.nsw.gov.au/npws.nsf/content/gliding+possums

www.deh.gov.au/biodiversity/threatened/publications/south–mole.html

www.nationalparks.nsw.gov.au/npws.nsf/content/bandicoots

www.parks.tas.gov.au/wildlife/mammals/bandicoot.html

www.easterbilby.com.au/save_bilby/chocolate.asp

www.calm.wa.gov.au/plants_animals/odd_bilby.html

www.deh.gov.au/biodiversity/threatened/publications/tsd05greater–bilby.html

www.amonline.net.au/archive.cfm?id=1692

www.naturalworlds.org/thylacine/

www.life.sci.qut.edu.au/timms/

www.savethekoala.com/

www.unep.org/geo2000/english/0045.htm

www.ucmp.berkeley.edu/mammal/monotremes.html

GLOSSARY

adaptive radiation–the process by which one species evolves into a number of other species that fill different niches in the environment.

arthropod–an animal's hard shell, or exoskeleton. Arthropods include insects, crabs, scorpions, centipedes, and spiders.

Australasia–the region of the earth consisting of Australia, Papua New Guinea, and nearby islands.

canid–a member of the dog family.

continental drift–the slow movement of Earth's continents.

convergent evolution–the process of two unrelated organisms evolving to have very similar features or habits.

embryon–the partially formed organism that a marsupial mother gives birth to; after it leaves the womb, the embryon attaches to the mother's nipple and continues to grow until it becomes a fully formed baby.

embryonic diapause–the ability of some marsupials to delay or "pause" the development of an embryo until the death or weaning of older offspring.

eucalyptus–plants native to Australasia. They are typically tough, woody plants that are hard to digest.

eutherian–the largest group of mammals. They are characterized by giving birth to fully formed babies; humans, dogs, and cats are eutherian.

evolution–the process that leads to change in life forms and the creation of new species over time. These changes result from changes in organisms' DNA.

family–a scientific grouping of closely related animals, plants, or other organisms. See: *Order*

fossil–the preserved remains of an organism that lived long ago.

Gondwana–an ancient supercontinent that consisted of present-day South America, Africa, Antarctica, India, and Australia. Also called *Gondwanaland*.

greenhouse gases–gases such as carbon dioxide and carbon monoxide that trap heat in Earth's atmosphere.

hallux–the opposable "big toe" on many marsupials that functions like a thumb.

invertebrate–any animal without a backbone.

joey–a baby marsupial, especially macropods and other pouched marsupials.

Laurasia–an ancient supercontinent that consisted of modern-day North America, Asia, and Europe.

marsupial–a mammal characterized by giving birth to partially formed babies. Also called a *metatherian*.

metatherian–a marsupial.

mob–a group kangaroos.

monotreme–an egg-laying mammal, such as the platypus or echidna.

omnivorous–capable of eating a wide variety of foods, both plant and animal material.

order–a scientific grouping of related animals that is larger than a family; several families may be contained in one order.

palate–the roof of the mouth of mammals and other vertebrates.

patagium–the loose fold of skin that gliding animals use as a wing or airfoil.

placenta–the organ in many mammals that allows a mother to pass nutrients and oxygen to an embryo growing inside of her.

prehensile–capable of grasping.

reproductive diapause–see *embryonic diapause*.

scent marking–leaving behind certain odor-producing substances; scent marking allows many mammals to mark out territories and communicate with potential intruders or mates.

speciation–the creation of new species through the process of evolution.

supercontinent–an ancient continent that consisted of several of our modern-day continents connected together. See: *Gondwana* and *Laurasia*.

syndactl–having one or more toes or fingers joined together; in species of the marsupial order Diprotodontia, the second and third toes of the hind foot are joined, or syndactl.